W9-AFU-208

# Jet Fighters microfacts

tangerine press

This book was conceived and produced by Design Eye Publishing
Project Editor: Corrine Ochiltree
Art Director: Danny Pyne

Co-ordinated and edited by Tall Tree Ltd
Text by Jon Richards
Design layout by Ben Ruocco
Picture Research by Lorna Ainger
Illustrations by Hardlines Ltd
Americanization by Jenny Siklos

First published in 2003 by Design Eye Publishing Ltd.
Copyright © 2003 Design Eye Holdings Limited
All rights reserved.

Scholastic and Tangerine Press and associated logos are trademarks of
Scholastic Inc
Published by Tangerine Press
an imprint of Scholastic Inc
557 Broadway; New York, NY 10012
10 9 8 7 6 5 4 3 2 1
ISBN 0–439–62756–7

Manufactured in China

Picture credits:
The publishers would like to thank the following for their kind permission
to reproduce their photographs:
Courtesy Martin-Baker Aircraft Company Ltd: 42
Corbis: 34t, Aero Graphics, Inc. 27t, David Blattel 34b, George Hall FC,
16–17b, 24–25b, 28b, 35, Museum of Flight 25t, Peter Russell/The Military
Picture Library 21t
Hulton Getty: 6b, 17t
PA Photos: EPA FC, 19t, 38b, 39t, Tim Ockendon 33t
Rex Features: Sipa Press BC 32c
TRH Pictures: 1, 5b, 7t, 8, 10, 18–19, 20b, 26–27b, 29t, 40–41b, 43
©Mark Wagner.aviation-images.com: 11, 41t, 46b, 47

4   Jet Fighters Introduction
6   Dawn of the Jet
8   Inside a Jet Engine
10  Pilot Training
12  Around an F-14 Tomcat
14  Around a Harrier
16  Clash of the Jets
18  Get Up and Go
20  Wing Shape
22  Around a Tornado
24  Cold War Fighters
26  Firing Weapons
28  Mission Profile
30  Around an F-16 Fighting Falcon
32  Navy Fighters
34  Flying the Plane
36  Around an F-117A Nighthawk
38  Modern Fighters
40  Ground Attack
42  Pilot Safety
44  Around a Joint Strike Fighters
46  Future Fighters
48  Glossary

# Jet Fighters
# Introduction

**Welcome to the ear-blasting, stomach-churning, white-knuckle world of jet fighters.**

This book will tell you the story of how the jet fighter was invented and how it has developed over the past 60 years into today's ultra-sophisticated flying machines

Read all about the most important fighter jets from around the world, find out how they have changed the face of modern warfare, and learn about all of the important facts and figures, including the wing span, the power of the engines and what kind of a punch they can pack in an air battle.

Once you learn about the world's best jets, build your very own fighters with four fantastic models at the back of this book. Simply pop the parts out from the sheets and follow the simple instructions to create your very own miniature air force. Then you and your friends can recreate breathtaking, all-action, jet-fighter dogfights.

# Dawn of
# *the Jet*

**During World War II (1939–1945), the throb of propeller aircraft started to be replaced by the roar of jets.**
Although they arrived too late to make an enormous impact on the war itself, these new aircraft were to change the face of air combat forever.

*Gloster Meteor* Although the Meteor entered service at the same time as the Me 262, it was never involved in combat. However, it did prove to be successful in bringing down large numbers of the V–1 flying bombs during the latter months of the war.

**Messerschmitt Me 262** Also called the Schwalbe ("swallow"), this jet was the only one to see air combat during World War II. It first flew in April 1941, but its introduction was held up by problems with the reliability of the Junkers jet engine, and it did not see action until July 1944.

Although jet fighters never actually fought each other during World War II, several of the countries involved in the conflict produced their own models. As well as the British Gloster Meteor and the German Messerschmitt Me 262 shown here, the Germans also produced the Heinkel He 280, and the U.S. produced the Bell P–59A.

## Father of the Jet

The man responsible for inventing the jet engine faced a long battle before his invention got off the ground. Frank Whittle first patented his jet design in 1930 and tested the world's first jet engine in 1937. But the British government and Air Force ignored the idea. Their minds changed with the outbreak of World War II.

# Inside a
# *Jet Engine*

**Although they are very complex machines, jet engines work on very simple principles.**
They work by sucking air into them, mixing it with a fine spray of aviation fuel, and then igniting it. This produces very hot gases that expand violently and roar out of the back of the engine in a jet, pushing the plane forward at the same time.

*Air intakes* Jet engines need to suck in huge amounts of air in order to work. Most modern fighter jets have the engines inside the main body, or fuselage. As a result, they need to have large air intakes underneath or on either side.

**Hot jet** Once on fire, the hot gases expand rapidly and force their way out of the back of the engine, creating the force that pushes the jet forward. This pushing force is called thrust.

**Fuel and air** Inside the engine, the air is squashed, or compressed, by the turbines, fuel is added, and the mixture is set on fire.

**Turbine blades** This kind of jet engine is a turbojet. It has a series of turbines, or bladed wheels. As these spin around, they force air into the engine.

## Other Kinds of Jets

A turbofan engine is similar to a turbojet, except that it has an enormous fan on the front. This is sent spinning by the jet blast from the back of the engine and produces most of the engine's thrust. A turboprop has a small propeller on the front that is also spun by the gases shooting out of the rear of the engine.

# Pilot Training

**It will take years before a pilot is qualified enough to fly one of today's jet fighters.**

Even before they've set foot in an aircraft, there are many months of theory lessons to learn. From there, a pilot will start on simple training aircraft, usually propeller-driven, before being allowed to fly a jet.

*Lesson time* A large proportion of a pilot's training is spent in lessons and lectures. Here, pilots are taught about all aspects of flying, from combat tactics to meteorology.

**_Feel the force_** During a mission, a pilot might be forced to make tight turns. This can be deadly, as high g-forces can force blood away from the head, causing the pilot to black out. To prepare them to cope with this, pilots train in a centrifuge. This huge spinning device recreates the high g-forces, allowing the pilot to practice ways to keep from blacking out.

## Survival Skills

Being a fighter pilot can mean that you are flying over enemy territory or deserted areas. Fighter pilots are therefore trained in survival techniques in case they are forced to crash. A rescue attempt might not be able to reach a crashed pilot for several days, so he or she must learn to survive on basic survival rations and what they can catch.

# Around an
# *F-14 Tomcat*

**First flown in May 1971, the F–14 Tomcat uses swing wings to change its shape for different purposes.**

It was initially designed as a carrier–based interceptor, defending the fleet from attack, but since its introduction, it has seen action as a spotter, or reconnaissance aircraft, as well as a bomber.

200

### *Fighter and bomber*
Although designed originally as a fighter, the F–14 was also designed to carry up to 14,500 lbs. (6,600 kg) of bombs. It carried out this bomber role during the 1995 Bosnia campaign, dropping laser–guided bombs onto targets.

### *In tandem* Designers
of the F–14 Tomcat decided to put the pilot and co-pilot in a tandem seating arrangement, or one in front of the other.

**Swing wings** The wings on the F-14 can be unswept to an angle of 20 degrees at their widest, or swept back to an angle of 68 degrees when they are flush against the fuselage of the aircraft.

**Arresting wires** At the back of the F-14 is a hook. This is lowered when the jet comes in to land on a carrier. As it touches down, this hook catches on wires on the flight deck and slows the jet down.

200

00

**Armament**
One Vulcan 20 mm cannon
Six AIM-54 Phoenix missiles
Six AIM-7 Sparrow missiles
Four AIM-9 Sidewinder missiles

# F-14 Stats

| | |
|---|---|
| Wingspan | 64 ft. (19.5 m) unswept, 38 ft. (11.5 m) swept |
| Length | 62 ft. 7 in. (18.75 m) |
| Engine | Two turbofan engines with afterburners |
| Thrust | 2 x 27,000 lbs. (12,300 kg) |
| Max speed | 1,563 mph (2,500 km/h) |
| Crew | Two |

# Around a *Harrier*

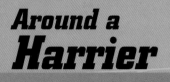

Now more than 40 years old, the Harrier jet is still the world's only vertical takeoff fighter aircraft. This fighter jet is able to take off and land vertically, hover in the air, and fly backward thanks to its ability to point the thrust from its engine in different directions, a system called thrust vectoring.

**Training missions**
Although a Harrier only has one crew member, special two-seater models were built for training missions, with pilot and co-pilot sitting one behind the other.

**Engine intakes**
Situated on either side of the pilot's cockpit are the enormous air intakes for the Harrier's engine.

**Moveable nozzles** The secret to the Harrier's hovering ability lies in the four moveable jet nozzles under the plane. For normal flight, these point backward, but are swiveled to point down when the pilot wants to hover.

**Forest clearings** Without the need for a long runway, Harriers can operate from a small clearing close to a front line.

**Armament**
One 25 mm cannon
Six Mk 82 500 lb. (227 kg) bombs
Or:
Four AIM-9 Sidewinder missiles

# Harrier Stats

| | |
|---|---|
| Wingspan | 30 ft. 3 in. (9 m) |
| Length | 46 ft. 3 in. (13.9 m) |
| Engine | One vectored thrust turbofan |
| Thrust | 22,200 lbs. (10,090 kg) |
| Max speed | 630 mph (1,008 km/h) |
| Crew | One |

# Clash of
# *The Jets*

## The period after World War II saw huge leaps in jet fighter technology.

This period saw the first supersonic jets as well as the first jet-on-jet combat action. Jet fighters clashed during the Korean war (1950–1953). Even though the F-86 Sabres of the U.S. Air Force and the MiG-15 used by the North Korean Air Force were evenly matched in terms of performance, there was little comparison in pilot training and ability.

**MiG-15** Looking remarkably similar to the Sabre, the MiG-15 had performance figures to match. It had a top speed of 668 mph (1,069 km/h) and packed a powerful punch with one machine gun and two cannons.

By the end of the war, 796 MiGs had been shot down and only 76 Sabres were lost.

**F-86 Sabre**
Incorporating several design features from the Messerschmitt Me 262 (see page 5), the first F-86 Sabre flew in October 1947. The finished fighter jet had an impressive array of weapons, including six machine guns and six rockets or bombs.

## Supersonic Flight

Since the end of World War II, aircraft designers had been trying to break the next hurdle in flight—to fly faster than sound. This was finally achieved by Chuck Yeager flying a rocket-powered Bell X-1A on October 14, 1947. Jet aircraft were not far behind matching this goal, and early prototypes of the F-86 Sabre broke the sound barrier.

# Get Up
# *and Go*

## How jets of hot gases leave a jet engine is just as important to a jet fighter as the amount of power produced.

This jet of hot gas can be directed to make the aircraft hover and perform remarkable aerobatic stunts.

> **Afterburners** When a lot of speed or acceleration is required, for example at takeoff, the pilot uses an afterburner. This dumps more fuel into the jet of already hot gases in the engine and sets the mixture on fire once again. This uses a lot of fuel, but creates a lot of speed.

**Thrust vectoring** While the Harrier jet deflects its thrust using swiveling nozzles (see pages 14–15), some jets use deflecting plates by their jet exhausts to push the thrust off to one side, such as this X–31 test plane. Thrust vectoring can create some spectacular maneuvers, such as allowing the aircraft to fly forward with its nose pointed up at an angle.

For some jets, however, a hot jet exhaust can be a problem. Some enemy sensors can detect the heat that a jet engine gives off. To overcome this, a stealth fighter will cool its jet exhausts to make them hard to detect.

## Cool Your Jets

Avoiding detection is vital to the F–117A Nighthawk, or Stealth Fighter (see pages 36–37). To escape detection by infrared sensors that would normally detect the heat from a jet's exhaust, the Nighthawk uses heat tiles similar to those on the Space Shuttle, and it also blows cold air onto its exhaust gases to cool things down.

# Wing *Shape*

Wings can come in all shapes and sizes, and designers have found that there is more than one kind of wing that is suitable for a fighter jet.

**Delta wings** Some fighter jets, such as this Mirage fighter, use a triangular wing, called a delta wing. This wing shape allows the jet to fly very fast to intercept enemy aircraft.

A modern fighter jet can have swept back wings, triangular wings, and wings that can even change their shape. Some experimental aircraft have even had wings that point forward, making them very unstable to fly, but extremely maneuverable.

**Swing wings**
Some fighters, such as the F-14 Tomcat (see pages 12–13) and the Tornado (see pages 22–23), are able to move their wings, effectively changing the shape of the aircraft to suit whether the pilots want to fly quickly or slowly.

## Swinging Wings

Known as variable geometry, the wings of a swing-wing aircraft are swung out to provide extra lift for slow flight, such as landing on an aircraft carrier. Swung back, they create a dart shape that is better for high speed and for flying faster than the speed of sound.

# Around a
# *Tornado*

**The Tornado was designed to replace Britain's Royal Air Force's Phantom fighters in the 1980s.**
Engineers and technicians created an aircraft that could fulfill a number of roles.

*Fighter and bomber* The Tornado has been adapted as both a fighter and a bomber. The latest fighter model is the F3, while the latest bomber model is called the GR4.

*Sharing information* The Tornado is equipped with a system that can gather information about a battle scene from other friendly aircraft. This allows pilots to pick a target and move into position without revealing their own position.

**Range** The fighter version of the Tornado can patrol for up to three hours and for up to 350 mi. (560 km) from its base before refueling.

**Longer and faster** The latest model of the Tornado fighter included a newly designed jet engine. Although these engines increased performance, designers had to stretch the length of the aircraft by 14 in. (36 cm) to fit them in.

**Armament**
One Mauser 27 mm cannon
Four AIM-120 missiles
Four AIM-9 Sidewinder missiles

# Tornado Stats

| | |
|---|---|
| Wingspan | 45 ft. 7 in. (13.9 m) unswept, 28 ft. (8.6 m) swept |
| Length | 61 ft. 3 in. (18.7 m) |
| Engine | Two afterburning turbofans |
| Thrust | 2 x 16,410 lbs. (7,460 kg) |
| Max speed | 1,480 mph (2,333 km/h) |
| Crew | Two |

# Cold War *Fighters*

The period after World War II and up to the 1990s was known as the Cold War. During this period, the U.S. and the U.S.S.R., along with their allies, faced each other in an uneasy peace. Both sides were involved in an escalating arms race, trying to build better and more weapons than the other side.

*F-4 Phantom* One of the most successful jet fighters ever built by the U.S., the Phantom first flew in 1958 and completed its last mission for the U.S. Air National Guard in 1995. During that time, it was involved in a wide range of missions, including air combat, interception, and ground support—as a bomber, the Phantom could carry more than twice the bomb load of a World War II B–17 bomber.

**Lightning** The English Electric Lightning was designed as a high-speed interceptor. It was capable of Mach 2.3—more than twice the speed of sound—and was equipped with two machine guns and could carry heat-seeking missiles.

The arms race saw an enormous technological leap in jet fighter performance and technology. Within 15 years of the end of World War II, jet fighters were being built that could reach twice the speed of sound and fire weapons that could destroy a target that was very far away.

## *Interceptors*

During the Cold War, aircraft from both sides flew close to, and sometimes entered, another country's airspace. In response, fast, supersonic jet fighters, such as the English Electric Lightning and the F-4 Phantom, were sent to intercept the intruders and escort them away.

# Firing
# *Weapons*

**Fighter jet weaponry has come a long way since the first air–to–air combat in World War I (1914–1918) when pilots fought with pistols and rifles.**

### *Ready for action*

Today's jet fighters can carry a massive array of weapons, packing more punch than an entire World War II squadron. This F/A–18 Hornet is equipped with two AIM–9 Sidewinder missiles on each wingtip and 10 AIM–120 missiles under the wings and fuselage. The Sidewinders are short–range air–to–air missiles, capable of hitting a target up to 18 mi. (29 km) away. The AIM–120s are medium–range air–to–air missiles that can be fired at a target that is 30 mi. (48 km) away.

*Air-to-air* The primary role of a fighter is to engage and destroy other aircraft. Today's jet fighters can detect and destroy other planes without even seeing it. Modern air-to-air missiles can be guided to a target either by heat-seeking sensors in the missile's tip that lock onto an aircraft's hot jet exhausts, or by radar equipment in the fighter.

Many of today's fighters are still equipped with guns, though they are more powerful machine guns and cannons. They also have hi-tech guided missile systems to attack targets far away.

## Hitting the Target

How a fighter jet engages a flying target depends on the kind of weapon it is going to use. A machine gun or cannon requires the pilot to line the aircraft up with the target. Heat-seeking missiles will lock onto the hot exhaust gases of the target, while radar guided missiles will use a radar beam to lock onto the target and guide it in.

# Mission
# *Profile*

**Whatever the kind of mission that fighter pilots have to fly, there are certain stages that each must go through every time.**

Preparation is vital for any mission, and pilots have to know what they are going to face and what weapons they can use. Once they are in the air, pilots need to navigate to various key points—perhaps to refuel or regroup with other aircraft.

*Takeoff* Once the pilots have been briefed, they can then prepare for the mission, put on their combat uniform, and then give their fighter a quick check. After that, they climb into their cockpit, taxi to the end of the runway, power up their engines, fire up the afterburners (see page 18), and take off into the sky.

**Refueling** Missions may involve spending long hours in the air, and fighter jets can guzzle huge amounts of fuel, especially if they use their afterburners. The trickiest part of a mission can be the midair refueling. A fighter pilot has to carefully maneuver the jet to within several feet of the tanker aircraft and engage with the refueling line. Fuel is then pumped into the fighter before the line is disengaged and the pilot can fly away.

Then they proceed to the target, and it is here that the pilot's skill becomes very important. Even though there may be a set plan about how to attack the target, the pilot has to deal with a number of things that might not have been planned for, such as the amount of antiaircraft fire. Once the target has been attacked, the pilot then has to complete the most important part of the mission—returning home safely.

## Briefing

Information is one of the most important factors in any military mission, and jet fighter pilots need to be briefed fully before going into action. During a briefing, pilots learn as much as possible about a mission, from weather conditions to the kind of target they might be facing, as well as the way they should handle it.

# Around an F-16
# *Fighting Falcon*

**Designed as a multi-role aircraft, the F-16 Fighting Falcon has become the world's most sought-after fighter.** Countries from all around the world have ordered nearly 5,000 of these jets that are capable of acting as fighters, bombers, and ground support planes.

*Bubble* The canopy of the cockpit is shaped like a bubble. This gives the pilot good visibility all around.

*Support* Designers of the F-16 angled the pilot seat back from the usual 13 degrees to 30 degrees. This increased the pilot's comfort and increased the level of g-forces he or she could tolerate.

*High gravity* The structure of the F-16 is lightweight but very strong. It can cope with forces nine times the force of gravity—more than any other fighter aircraft.

**Long-range** The F-16 can fly 500 mi. (860 km), deliver its weapons, defend itself from attack, and return to its base.

SW
256

**Fast fighter** The powerful jet engine can push the F-16 to Mach 2—that's twice the speed of sound.

**Armament**
One 20 mm cannon
Six AIM−9 Sidewinder missiles
Or:
Two 2,000 lb (900 kg) bombs
Two AIM−9 missiles

# F-16 Stats

| | |
|---|---|
| Wingspan | 32 ft. 8 in. (9.8 m) |
| Length | 49 ft. 5 in. (14.8 m) |
| Engine | One turbofan |
| Thrust | 29,000 lbs. (13,200 kg) |
| Max speed | 1,500 mph (2,400 km/h) |
| Crew | One |

# Navy
# *Fighters*

**Ever since the end of World War I, military chiefs have seen the importance of having aircraft based at sea.**

Today's naval aircraft provide airborne protection for a fleet, while the aircraft carriers they fly from act as mobile bases, allowing them to strike at a target in a matter of hours.

***Anti-ship*** As well as defending a fleet, fast-moving and small fighter jets have been effective at attacking ships. Flying close to the waves, they can avoid detection and fire anti-ship missiles a great distance from their target. This kind of attack was very effective during the Falklands War (1982) when Argentinian Mirage jets fired Exocet missiles (above) to destroy several British ships.

> **Sea Harrier** The Harrier's ability to take off from short runways and land vertically make it ideal as a carrier-based fighter. Using its swiveling nozzles (see page 15), it can take off on a very short runway, especially if there is a ramp at the end that can be used to boost the plane into the air.

However, being based at sea does have its problems. The aircraft carriers need to be enormous to house the equipment as well as the thousands of men and women needed to keep a squadron operational.

## Folding Wings

Space on an aircraft carrier is very important. Carrier aircraft need to be as small as possible so that they can all fit into the hangars that are below the flight deck. To help with this, many carrier aircraft have wings that can fold in half. Once the aircraft has landed, the wingtips can be folded up, making the fighter's size much smaller.

# Flying *the Plane*

**Today's fighter pilots have to deal with an enormous amount of information while flying the plane.** During a mission, they will be continuously bombarded with data from sensors and instruments both inside and outside the aircraft.

*Heads up* In order to keep the pilot's eyes forward and concentrating on what's important, information about the plane is projected on a center screen (see inset). This is called a Heads-Up Display, or HUD.

Part of a pilot's skill is dealing with information and flying the aircraft on its mission—as well as looking out for any enemy aircraft all at the same time.

## Fly-By-Wire

Modern fighter pilots control their aircraft using fly-by-wire technology. Here, computers and electronics move the plane's control surfaces, such as the flaps on the wings, in response to the pilot's movements in the cockpit. This system has replaced the wires and cables that linked the pilot's controls with the plane in old fighters.

# Around an F-117A
# *Nighthawk*

**Every aspect of this aircraft has been designed with one thing in mind— to avoid detection.**

From the unique body shape to the cooling of its jet exhausts (see page 19), the Nighthawk was the world's first true stealth aircraft.

**Doors** Any doors on the Nighthawk have jagged edges. These scatter radar signals better than doors with straight edges.

**Special paint** Technicians who built the Nighthawk created a special coating that was designed to absorb radar signals.

**Hidden cameras**
The plane's sensors are hidden inside ports in the fuselage.

**Butterfly** The Nighthawk uses these unusual butterfly-shaped tail fins that help scatter radar signals.

**Hidden weapons** All of the Nighthawk's weapons are stowed inside the weapons' bay so that no hard points stand out from the aircraft's surface and reflect radar signals.

**Body shape** The body of the Nighthawk is made up of a lot of flat, angular surfaces. These are designed to scatter any radar signals so that very few reflect back to anyone trying to find the fighter.

**Armament** Two laser-guided bombs

# Nighthawk Stats

| | |
|---|---|
| Wingspan | 43 ft. 4 in. (13.2 m) |
| Length | 65 ft. 11 in. (20.3 m) |
| Engine | Two turbofans |
| Thrust | 2 x 10,600 lbs. (4,820 kg) |
| Max speed | 646 mph (1,040 km/h) |
| Crew | One |

# Modern Fighters

Today's jet fighters use the very latest technology to create the most-advanced aircraft in the world. Space-age materials, such as carbon fiber composites and glass-reinforced plastic, are used in manufacturing to make the jets light and strong.

**Eurofighter** Designed and built by companies from several European countries, the Eurofighter Typhoon is one of the most advanced aircraft ever produced. Its delta wing (see page 20) design also has a small moveable wing in the front, called a canard. This orientation makes the fighter unstable in flight, but extremely maneuverable.

**F-22 Raptor** Aircraft designers have incorporated many of the stealth features used in the F-117A Nighthawk (see pages 36–37) in designing the F-22 Raptor. These include keeping the bulk of the Raptor's weapons housed in internal bays. This reduces its visibility to radar and also reduces drag on the aircraft, improving its range and performance.

Modern fighters also use the very latest weapons, including the JDAM (Joint Direct Attack Munitions) system, which can be connected to existing bombs and uses global positioning satellites to guide them to a target with pinpoint accuracy.

## Supercruise

Both the Eurofighter and the F-22 Raptor use engines that are capable of "supercruise." This means that they are able to fly at supersonic speeds (i.e. faster than the speed of sound), without using fuel-thirsty afterburners (see page 18). This reduces the heat produced by the jets, improving their stealth capabilities as well as their performance.

# Ground
# *Attack*

**Because of their high speed, small size, and great maneuverability, fighter jets also make the perfect aircraft for attacking ground targets.**

While they might not have the massive range of the enormous B-52 bombers, jet fighters are able to reach a target quickly, attack hard-to-reach targets, such as underground bunkers, and escape virtually undetected.

> ***Missiles or bombs*** As well as a wide range of air-to-air missiles, fighter jets can carry an enormous range of ground attack weapons, including guided bombs and missiles such as the AGM-65 Maverick missile.

**Before**

**After**

*Gun camera* These pictures taken by a fighter jet show just how effective a bombing mission can be. On the left is a bridge before an attack, and on the right is the same bridge afterward. With these photos, military leaders could see that the mission was a success and did not need to be repeated.

Knowledge is a very important factor in any attack, especially when attacking ground targets. It is vital to know where a target is and if an attack has been a success or not. Fighter jets are invaluable for gathering information, or reconnaissance, using cameras to take pictures of a target.

## Target Illumination

Not every aircraft attacking a ground target will be carrying a weapon. Some of them may be equipped with lasers that are aimed at the target to "illuminate" it. Guided bombs and missiles then follow the laser beam to exactly the right spot.

# *Pilot* *Safety*

One of the most delicate objects inside a jet fighter is the pilot, who must be protected at all costs. Without a pilot, the mission is a failure. Jet fighter designers have used several methods to protect pilots, including rocket-powered ejection seats.

> *Ejection seats* The fast speeds at which fighter jets travel mean the pilots have no time to climb out onto the wing and jump to safety as World War II pilots could. Instead, they use an ejection seat. With the pull of a lever, the glass canopy is blown clear and rockets on the pilot's seat blast the pilot and the seat clear of the aircraft, allowing the pilot to parachute to safety.

**Helmet** A fighter pilot's helmet offers some protection from the high gravitational forces of flying a combat aircraft as well as some noise protection. It also holds radio equipment, and a tinted visor reduces glare from the Sun.

**Mask** Oxygen is pumped to the pilot through the mask. At high altitudes, oxygen is very thin and the pilot needs this to survive.

**Survival vest** The pilot's survival vest contains tools and equipment that may become vital if a crash occurs. These include a radio beacon, camouflage paint, and flares.

**G-suit** Pilots wear g-suits that have inflatable air pockets inside them. These inflate to squeeze the legs and force blood into the upper body. This stops a pilot from "blacking out" during a tight turn.

## Zero-Zero

Modern ejection seats have what is called a "zero-zero" capability. This means that they work successfully when a plane is standing still on the ground and blast the pilot up to a safe height for the parachute to open.

# Around a Joint
# *Strike Fighter*

The Joint Strike Fighter (JSF), or F–35, is a truly unique aircraft. Three different models are being built that will provide three very different roles.

The U.S. Air Force model will be an aircraft that takes off and lands normally. The U.S. Navy will have a slightly different version to use on its carriers. Finally, the U.S. Marine Corps and the British Navy will have a version that is capable of short and vertical takeoff and landing to replace the Harrier (see pages 14–15).

**Armament**
Initial designs for the JSF have two weapons bays inside the aircraft that are located just in front of the landing gear. There are also plans for an external machine gun pod.

**Lift fan** At the center of the British Navy and Marine Corps model is a powerful lift fan. Doors above and below the fan open when the pilot wants to take off or land vertically, or to hover.

**Long distance**
The internal fuel tanks on the JSF can hold up to 16,000 lbs. (7,250 kg) of fuel.

**Supersonic** The powerful engine inside the JSF means that this will be the first supersonic aircraft that can land and take off vertically.

X-35

**Control surfaces** The JSF has much larger flaps and rudders than its predecessors. These bigger control surfaces make it easier to control the plane at slow speeds, such as when landing on an aircraft carrier.

# Joint Strike Fighter Stats

| | |
|---|---|
| Wingspan | 36 ft. (10.8 m) |
| Length | 45 ft. (13.5 m) |
| Engine | One turbofan |
| Thrust | 35,000 lbs. (15,910 kg) |
| Max speed | 1,000 mph (1,600 km/h) |
| Crew | One |

# *Future* **Fighters**

## In the 60 years since the first jets took to the skies, fighter design has changed incredibly.

Stealth technology has meant that fighter jets can patrol the skies undetected, making them virtually invisible to any kind of sensor. With fighter jet technology advancing so quickly, aircraft designers now have a new barrier to overcome—the pilot.

> ### *Experimental aircraft*
> Fighter jet designers are always trying to test the limits of aircraft technology. The X–36 aircraft, for example, has no horizontal stabilizer, making it unstable during flight, but very maneuverable.

Technology has almost made the pilot's role redundant, and increases in jet fighter speed and performance are sometimes held up by a pilot's inability to cope with the physical exertion required.

# X-Planes

Since it was formed in the 1950s, the National Aeronautic and Space Administration (NASA) has built a series of experimental planes, called the X-planes. Over the years, these aircraft have tested new technologies, such as lifting bodies, thrust vectoring, and forward-swept wings.

# Glossary

**Afterburner**
A system to boost the thrust of a jet engine, where extra fuel is pumped into the engine and set on fire again to create a surge of power.

**Canards**
Small, moveable wings at the front of a plane that can be moved by the pilot to alter the plane's course.

**Canopy**
The glass and metal bubble that covers the pilot and the cockpit.

**Cockpit**
The part of the plane where the pilot sits and where the controls are found.

**Control surfaces**
These are the moveable parts found on the wings and horizontal stabilizers, such as the flaps and the rudder. The pilot can move these using the controls in order to alter the course of the plane.

**G-forces**
The forces of gravity that act upon a pilot during a flight. In a tight turn, or under high acceleration, these g-forces can be so extreme that a pilot may black out.

**Supersonic**
Faster than the speed of sound.

**Thrust**
The pushing force that moves a jet fighter forward. The thrust in a jet is produced by setting a mixture of fuel and air on fire. As they burn, they produce hot gases that expand and blast out of the back of a jet engine, pushing it forward at the same time.

**Thrust vectoring**
Deflecting the thrust's path to produce maneuvers such as hovering and vertical takeoff.

**Turbines**
Bladed wheels found inside jet engines.